FLIPBOOK

EIFFEL

TOWER

Jean Knoertzer

The **Eiffel Tower** is a wrought-iron lattice tower on the Champ de Mars in Paris, France. It is named after the engineer Gustave Eiffel, whose company designed and built the tower.

Constructed from 1887 to 1889 as the entrance to the 1889 World's Fair, it was initially criticised by some of France's leading artists and intellectuals for its design, but it has become a global cultural icon of France and one of the most recognisable structures in the world.

The tower is 324 metres (1,063 ft) tall, about the same height as an 81-storey building, and the tallest structure in Paris. Its base is square, measuring 125 metres (410 ft) on each side. During its construction, the Eiffel Tower surpassed the Washington Monument to become the tallest man-made structure in the world, a title it held for 41 years until the Chrysler Building in New York

City was finished in 1930. It was the first structure to reach a height of 300 metres. Due to the addition of a broadcasting aerial at the top of the tower in 1957, it is now taller than the Chrysler Building by 5.2 metres (17 ft). Excluding transmitters, the Eiffel Tower is the second tallest free-standing structure in France after the Millau Viaduct.

The tower has three levels for visitors, with restaurants on the first and second levels. The top level's upper platform is 276 m (906 ft) above the ground – the highest observation deck accessible to the public in the European Union. Tickets can be purchased to ascend by stairs or lift to the first and second levels. The climb from ground level to the first level is over 300 steps, as is the climb from the first level to the second. Although there is a staircase to the top level, it is usually accessible only by lift.

he design of the Eiffel Tower is attributed to Maurice Koechlin and Émile Nouguier, two senior engineers working for the Compagnie des Établissements Eiffel. It was envisioned after discussion about a suitable centrepiece for the proposed 1889 Exposition Universelle, a world's fair to celebrate the centennial of the French Revolution. Eiffel openly acknowledged that inspiration for a tower came from the Latting Observatory built in New York City in 1853. In May 1884, working at home, Koechlin made a sketch of their idea, described by him as "a great pylon, consisting of four lattice girders standing apart at the base and coming together at the top, joined together by metal trusses at regular intervals". Eiffel initially showed little enthusiasm, but he did approve further study, and the two engineers then asked Stephen Sauvestre, the head of company's architectural department, to contribute to the design. Sauvestre added decorative arches to the base of the tower, a glass pavilion to the first level, and other embellishments.

The new version gained Eiffel's support: he bought the rights to the patent on the design which Koechlin, Nougier, and Sauvestre had taken out, and the design was exhibited at the Exhibition of Decorative Arts in the autumn of 1884 under the company name. On 30 March 1885, Eiffel presented his plans to the *Société des Ingénieurs Civils*; after discussing the technical problems and emphasising the practical uses of the tower, he finished his talk by saying the tower would symbolise, not only the art of the modern engineer, but also the century of Industry and Science in which we are living, and for which the way was prepared by the great scientific movement of the eighteenth century and by the Revolution of 1789, to which this monument will be built as an expression of France's gratitude.

Little progress was made until 1886, when Jules Grévy was re-elected as president of France and Édouard Lockroy was appointed as minister for trade. A budget for the exposition was passed and, on 1 May, Lockroy announced an alteration to the terms of the open competition being held for a centrepiece to the exposition, which effectively made the selection of Eiffel's design a foregone conclusion, as entries had to include a study for a 300 m (980 ft) four-sided metal tower on the Champ de Mars. (A 300-meter tower was then considered a herculean engineering effort). On 12 May, a commission was set up to examine Eiffel's scheme and its rivals, which, a month later, decided that all the proposals except Eiffel's were either impractical or lacking in details.

After some debate about the exact location of the tower, a contract was signed on 8 January 1887. This was signed by Eiffel acting in his own capacity rather than as the representative of his company, and granted him 1.5 million francs toward the construction costs: less than a quarter of the estimated 6.5 million francs. Eiffel was to receive all income from the commercial exploitation of the tower during the exhibition and for the next 20 years. He later established a separate company to manage the tower, putting up half the necessary capital himself.

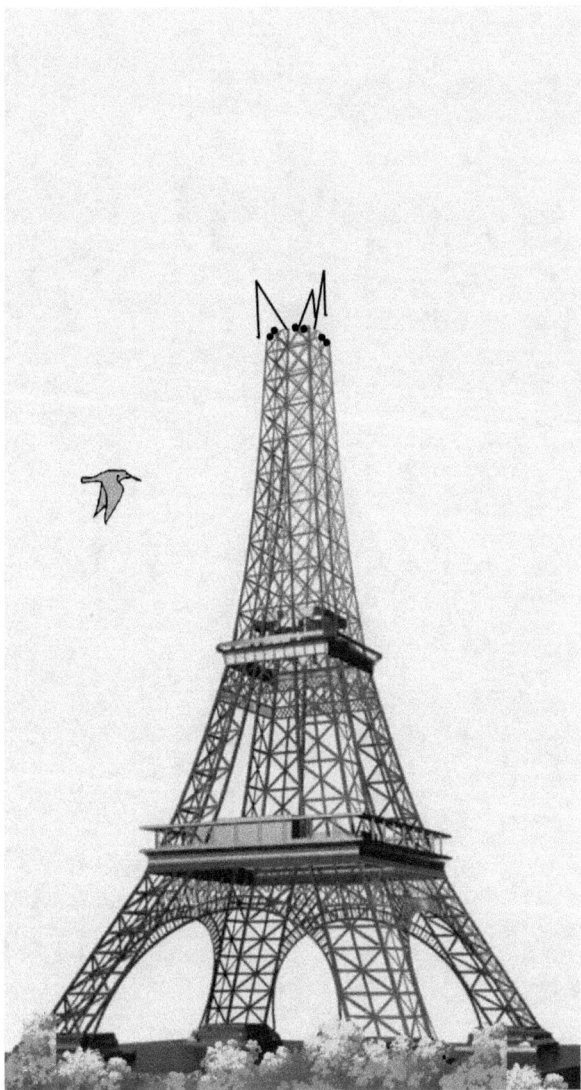

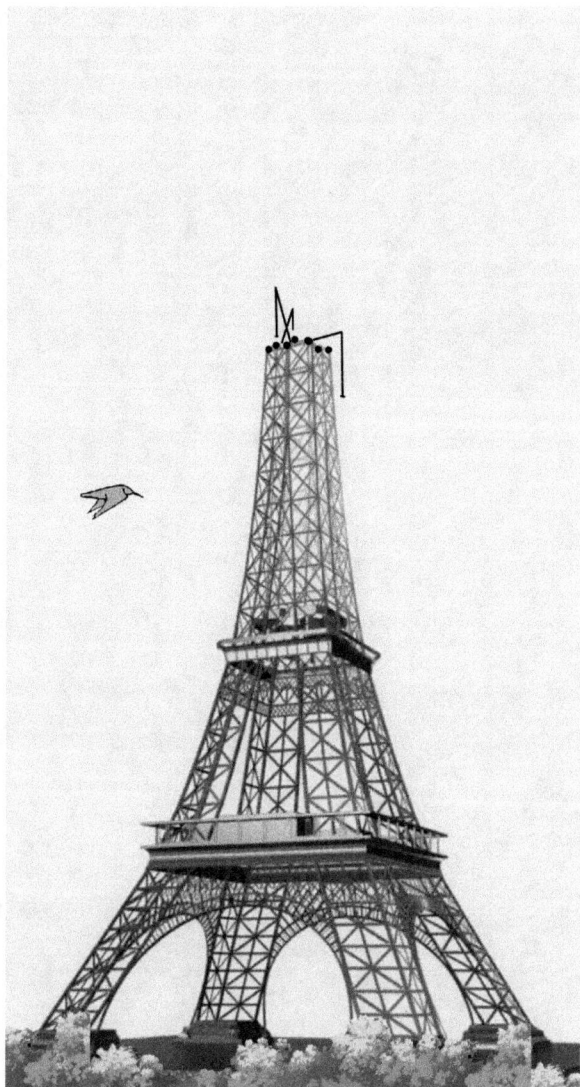

www.ingramcontent.com/pod-product-compliance
Lightning Source LLC
LaVergne TN
LVHW051639080426
835511LV00016B/2391